M

Quotes & Facts

Annotated by Blago Kirov

First Edition

*****

Mao Zedong: Quotes & Facts
*****

Copyright © 2019 Annotations by Blago Kirov

Foreword

"Political power grows out of the barrel of a gun."

Mao Zedong or Mao Tse-tung was a Chinese revolutionary, politician, and author. As chairman of the Communist Party of China (1943-1976), chairman of the Central People's Government (1949-1954) and chairman of the People's Republic of China (1954-1959), he was the leading politician who governed the People's Republic of China he founded from 1949 to 1976. The Maoist political movement is named after him.

Influenced by the Xinhai Revolution of 1911, which created the Republic of China, the movement of May 4, 1919 and his student days, Mao was a founding member of the Communist Party and the Red Army, which fought against Kuomintang troops in the Chinese Civil War (1927-1949) and won and established the People's Republic of China shortly after the united front of the Second Japanese-Chinese War.

After its takeover, China's transformation from a backward agricultural feudal state to a political and economic superpower began.

On the other hand, Mao's campaigns and programs, especially the Great Leap Forward and the Cultural Revolution, resulted in the deaths of tens of millions of people, sometimes catastrophic economic damage, huge losses of cultural heritage and dramatic upheaval of social structures. Victims of up to 45 million deaths between 1958 and 1962 are assumed as a result of Mao's policies. The Chinese-American economist and Marxist Li Minqi justify Mao with the argument that the Great Leap Forward had catastrophic consequences, but at the same time created the infrastructure to prevent later economic crises.

Under Deng Xiaoping, Mao's principles were substantially abandoned in China after 1976 as part of the reform and opening policy. Nevertheless, his legacy as an important revolutionary, military strategist and political leader continues to be honored. Among other things, he is depicted on Chinese banknotes and in a prominent place at the Gate of Heavenly Peace, where he proclaimed the People's Republic of China on 1 October 1949.

Despite the controversies still surrounding him, Mao is regarded as one of the most influential politicians in history and was named one of the 100 most important people of the 20th century by Time Magazine in 1998.

His Words

The great man, Genghis Khan, only knew how to shoot eagles with an arrow. The past is past. To see real heroes, look around you.
Qinyuanchun (1936; first published in late 1945

What we need is an enthusiastic but calm state of mind, and intense but orderly work.
"Problems of Strategy in China's Revolutionary War", (December 1936)

Where there is oppression, there is revolt.
In Edgar Snow's Red Star over China (1937)

I knew the Classics, but disliked them. What I enjoyed were the romances of Old China, and especially stories of rebellions. I read the Yo Fei Chuan, Shui Hu Chuan, Fan T'ang, San Kuo, and Hsi Yu Chi, while still very young, and despite the vigilance of my old teacher, who hated these outlawed books and called them wicked.
In Edgar Snow's Red Star over China (1937)

We should support whatever our enemies oppose and oppose whatever our enemies support.
Quotation from Chairman Mao Zedong (The Little Red Book)

A revolution is not a dinner party, or writing an essay, or painting a picture, or doing embroidery. It cannot be so refined, so leisurely and gentle, so temperate, kind, courteous, restrained and magnanimous. A revolution is an insurrection, an act of violence by which one class overthrows another.
Quotation from Chairman Mao Zedong (The Little Red Book)

Every Communist must grasp the truth: Political power grows out of the barrel of a gun.
Quotation from Chairman Mao Zedong (The Little Red Book)

All reactionaries are paper tigers. In appearance, the reactionaries are terrifying, but in reality they are not so powerful. From a long-term point of view, it is not the reactionaries but the people who are really powerful.
Quotation from Chairman Mao Zedong (The Little Red Book)

The revolutionary war is a war of the masses; it can be waged only by mobilizing the masses and relying on them.
Quotation from Chairman Mao Zedong (The Little Red Book)

If the U.S. monopoly capitalist groups persist in pushing their policies of aggression and war, the day is bound to come when they will be hanged by the people of the whole world. The same fate awaits the accomplices of the United States.
Quotation from Chairman Mao Zedong (The Little Red Book)

There is an ancient Chinese fable called "The Foolish Old Man Who Removed the Mountains". It tells of an old man who lived in northern China long, long ago and was known as the Foolish Old Man of North Mountain. His house faced south and beyond his doorway stood the two great peaks, Taihang and Wangwu, obstructing the way. He called his sons, and hoe in hand they began to dig up these mountains with great determination. Another graybeard, known as the Wise Old Man, saw them and said derisively, "How silly of you to do this! It is quite impossible for you few to dig up those two huge mountains." The Foolish Old Man replied, "When I die, my sons will carry on; when they die, there will be my grandsons, and then their sons and grandsons, and so on to infinity. High as they are, the mountains cannot grow any higher and with every bit we dig, they will be that much lower. Why can't we clear them away?" Having refuted the Wise Old Man's wrong view, he went on digging every day, unshaken in his conviction. God was moved by this, and he sent down two angels, who carried the mountains away on their backs. Today, two big mountains lie like a dead weight on the Chinese people. One is imperialism, the other is feudalism. The Chinese Communist Party has long made up its mind to dig them up. We must persevere and work unceasingly, and we, too, will touch God's heart. Our God is none other than the masses of the Chinese people. If they stand up and dig together with us, why can't these two mountains be cleared away?
The Foolish Old Man Who Removed the Mountains (1945)

Without a People's army, the people have nothing.

Quotation from Chairman Mao Zedong (The Little Red Book)

Our principle is that the Party commands the gun, and the gun must never be allowed to command the Party.
Quotation from Chairman Mao Zedong (The Little Red Book)

Be resolute, fear no sacrifice and surmount every difficulty to win victory.
Quotation from Chairman Mao Zedong (The Little Red Book)

Liberalism is extremely harmful in a revolutionary collective. It is a corrosive which eats away unity, undermines cohesion, causes apathy and creates dissension. It robs the revolutionary ranks of compact organization and strict discipline, prevents policies from being carried through and alienates the Party organizations from the masses which the Party leads. It is an extremely bad tendency.
Quotation from Chairman Mao Zedong (The Little Red Book)

Our purpose is to ensure that literature and art fit well into the whole revolutionary machine as a component part, that they operate as powerful weapons for uniting and educating the people and for attacking and destroying the enemy, and that they help the people fight the enemy with one heart and one mind.
Quotation from Chairman Mao Zedong (The Little Red Book)

In the ideological field, the question of who will win in the struggle between the proletariat and the bourgeoisie has not been really settled yet. We still have to wage a protracted struggle against bourgeois and petty bourgeois ideology. It is wrong not to understand this and to give up ideological struggle. All erroneous ideas, all poisonous weeds, all ghosts and monsters, must be subjected to criticism; in no circumstance should they be allowed to spread unchecked. However, the criticism should be fully reasoned, analytical and convincing, and not rough, bureaucratic, metaphysical or dogmatic.
Quotation from Chairman Mao Zedong (The Little Red Book)

Many people think it impossible for guerrillas to exist for long in the enemy's rear. Such a belief reveals lack of comprehension of the relationship that should exist between the people and the troops. The former may be likened to water the latter to the fish who inhabit it. How may it be said that these two cannot exist together?
On Guerilla Warfare (1937), Chapter 6

This is usually aphorized as "The people are the sea that the revolutionary swims in," or an equivalent.
On Protracted War, May 1938

Politics is war without bloodshed, while war is politics with bloodshed.
On Protracted War, May 1938

Marxism comprises many principles, but in the final analysis they can all be brought back to a single sentence: it is right to rebel.

Speech marking the 60th birthday of Stalin (20 December 1939)

The atom bomb is a paper tiger which the U.S. reactionaries use to scare people. It looks terrible but in fact it isn't. Of course, the atom bomb is a weapon of mass slaughter, but the outcome of a war is decided by the people--not by one of two new types of weapon.
Talk with the American Correspondent Anna Louise Strong (August 1946)

"You are dictatorial." My dear sirs, you are right, that is just what we are. All the experience the Chinese people have accumulated through several decades teaches us to enforce the people's democratic dictatorship, that is, to deprive the reactionaries of the right to speak and let the people alone have that right.
The People's Democratic Dictatorship, speech (30 June 1949) commemorating the 28th anniversary of the Chinese Communist Party

Democracy is practiced within the ranks of the people, who enjoy the rights of freedom of speech, assembly, association and so on. The right to vote belongs only to the people, not to the reactionaries. The combination of these two aspects, democracy for the people and dictatorship over the reactionaries, is the people's democratic dictatorship.
"On the People's Democratic Dictatorship" (1949)

The people's state protects the people. Only when the people have such a state can they educate and remold themselves by democratic methods on a country-wide scale, with everyone taking part, and shake off the influence of domestic and foreign reactionaries...rid themselves of the bad habits and ideas acquired in the old society, not allow themselves to be led astray by the reactionaries, and continue to advance- to advance towards a socialist and communist society.
"On the People's Democratic Dictatorship" (1949)

As for members of the reactionary classes and individuals so long as they do not rebel, sabotage or create trouble after their political power has been overthrown, land and work will be given to them as well in order to allow them to live and remold themselves through labor into new people. If they are not willing to work, the people's state will compel them to work. Propaganda and educational work will be done among them too and will be done, moreover, with as much care and thoroughness as among the captured army officers in the past.
"On the People's Democratic Dictatorship" (1949)

Stalin made mistakes. He made mistakes towards us, for example, in 1927. He made mistakes towards the Yugoslavs too. One cannot advance without mistakes... It is necessary to make mistakes. The party cannot be educated without learning from mistakes. This has great significance.
Said to Enver Hoxha, on his visit to China in 1956

There are a lot of things we can learn from the Soviet Union. Naturally, we should learn from its advanced and not its backward experience. The slogan we have advocated all along is to draw on the advanced Soviet experience. Who told you to pick up its backward experience? Some people are so undiscriminating that they say a Russian fart is fragrant. That too is subjectivism. The Russians themselves say it stinks. Therefore, we should be analytical.
Strengthen Party Unity and Carry Forward Party Traditions (30 August 1956)

"Let a hundred flowers bloom; let a hundred schools of thought contend" is the policy for promoting progress in the arts and the sciences and a flourishing socialist culture in our land.
Slogan used at the start of the Hundred Flowers Campaign of open criticism of the communist government that began in late 1956 and ended in July 1957.

Ours is a people's democratic dictatorship, led by the working class and based on the worker-peasant alliance.
On the Correct Handling of Contradiction (1957)

Criticisms from democratic personages can be of only two kinds, those that are wrong and those that are not. Criticisms that are not wrong can help remedy our shortcomings while wrong ones must be refuted. As for such types as Liang Shu-ming, Peng Yi-hu and Chang Nai-chi, if they want to fart, let them. That will be to our advantage, for everybody can judge whether the smell is good or foul, and through discussion the majority can be won over and these types isolated.

Talk at a Conference of Secretaries of Provincial, Municipal and Autonomous Region Party Committees (27 January 1957)

Strategically we should despise all our enemies, while tactically we should take them all seriously.
Speech in Moscow at the meeting of Communist and Workers Parties of Socialist Countries (18 November 1957)

If we did ten things, nine were bad and got disclosed by the newspapers, we will be over. Then I will go, to the countryside, lead the peasant and revolt. If the Liberation Army do not follow me, I will get the Red Army.)
Speech at the Lushan Conference (23 July 1959)

The chaos caused was on a grand scale and I take responsibility. Comrades, you must all analyze your own responsibility. If you have to shit, shit! If you have to fart, fart! You will feel much better for it.
Speech at The Lushan Conference (23 July 1959)

Maybe you're afraid of sinking. Don't think about it. If you don't think about it, you won't sink. If you do, you will.
Swimming advice to physician Zhisui Li (1966)

There are many stubborn elements, graduates in the specialty schools of stubbornness (Referring to the Kuomintang). They are stubborn today, they will be stubborn tomorrow, and they will be stubborn the day after tomorrow. What is stubbornness (wan gu)? "Gu" is to be stiff. "Wan" is to not progress: not today, nor tomorrow, nor the day after tomorrow. People like that are called the "stubborn elements". It is not an easy thing to make the stubborn elements listen to our words.
Mao, 1967, as quoted by Jing Huang in The Role of Government Propaganda in the Educational System during the Cultural Revolution in China.

All the rest of the world uses the word "electricity." They've borrowed the word from English. But we Chinese have our own word for it!
Khrushchev Remembers (1970), p. 474

People who try to commit suicide — don't attempt to save them! . . . China is such a populous nation, it is not as if we cannot do without a few people.
Mao's Last Revolution (2006)

Children are the masters of the new society.
Decree Regarding Marriage (January 28, 1931)

Racial discrimination in the United States is a product of the colonialist and imperialist system. The contradiction between the Black masses in the United States and the U.S. ruling circles is a class contradiction. Only by overthrowing the reactionary rule of the U.S. monopoly capitalist class and destroying the colonialist and imperialist system can the Black people in the United States win complete emancipation. The Black masses and the masses of white working people in the United States have common interests and common objectives to struggle for. Therefore, the Afro-American struggle is winning sympathy and support from increasing numbers of white working people and progressives in the United States. The struggle of the Black people in the United States is bound to merge with the American workers' movement, and this will eventually end the criminal rule of the U.S. monopoly capitalist class.
"A New Storm against Imperialism" (1968)

My closest friend and brother – this world is lucky to have a great personality as Kim Il Sung. This causes my boundless happiness. The fate of the world revolution and the international communist movement are on your shoulders, Comrade Kim Il Sung. I wish you long life and good health.
Association for the Study of Songun Politics UK

Why must there be a revolutionary party? There must be a revolutionary party because the world contains enemies who oppress the people and the people want to throw off enemy oppression. In the era of capitalism and imperialism, just such a revolutionary party as the Communist Party is needed. Without such a party it is simply impossible for the people to throw off enemy oppression. We are Communists, we want to lead the people in overthrowing the enemy, and so we must keep our ranks in good order, we must march in step, our troops must be picked troops and our weapons good weapons. Without these conditions the enemy cannot be overthrown.
"Rectify the Party's Style of Work" (1942)

Subjectivism, sectarianism and stereotyped Party writing are no longer the dominant styles, but merely gusts of contrary wind, ill winds from the air-raid tunnels.
"Rectify the Party's Style of Work" (1942)

What is knowledge? Ever since class society came into being the world has had only two kinds of knowledge, knowledge of the struggle of production and knowledge of the class struggle. Natural science and social science are the crystallization of these two kinds of knowledge, and philosophy is the generalization and summation of the knowledge of nature.
"Rectify the Party's Style of Work" (1942)

I am hated by many, especially comrade Peng Dehuai, his hatred is so intense that he wished me dead. My policy with Peng Dehuai is such: You don't touch me, I don't touch you; You touch me, I touch you. Even though we were once like brothers, it doesn't change a thing.
"A Single Spark Can Start a Prairie Fire" (January 5, 1930)

When we look at a thing, we must examine its essence and treat its appearance merely as an usher at the threshold, and once we cross the threshold, we must grasp the essence of the thing; this is the only reliable and scientific method of analysis.
"A Single Spark Can Start a Prairie Fire" (January 5, 1930)

In approaching a problem a Marxist should see the whole as well as the parts. A frog in a well says, "The sky is no bigger than the mouth of the well." That is untrue, for the sky is not just the size of the mouth of the well. If it said, "A part of the sky is the size of the mouth of a well", that would be true, for it tallies with the facts.
"On Tactics Against Japanese Imperialism" (December 27, 1935)

We the Chinese nation have the spirit to fight the enemy to the last drop of our blood, the determination to recover our lost territory by our own efforts, and the ability to stand on our own feet in the family of nations.
"On Tactics Against Japanese Imperialism" (December 27, 1935)

Active defense is also known as offensive defense, or defense by decisive battles. Passive defense is also known as purely defensive defense or pure defense. Passive defense is actually a sham defense; active defense is the only real defense, the only defense for the purpose of counter-attacking and taking the offensive. As far as I known, there is no military manual of any value, nor is there any reasonably intelligent military expert, ancient or modern, Chinese or foreign, that does not oppose passive defense, strategically or tactically. Only the greatest fool or madman would hold up passive defense as a magic weapon.
Mao's Road to Power: Revolutionary Writings, 1912-49: v. 5

All relatively complete knowledge is formed in two stages: the first stage is perceptual knowledge, the second is rational knowledge, the latter being the development of the former to a higher stage.
"Rectify the Party's Style of Work" (1942)

Who are the honest people? Marx, Engels, Lenin and Stalin are honest, men of science are honest. Which are the dishonest people? Trotsky, Bukharin, Chen Tu-hsiu, and Chang Kuo-tao are extremely dishonest; and those who assert "independence" out of personal or sectional interest are dishonest too.
"Rectify the Party's Style of Work" (1942)

We must build a centralized, unified Party and make a clean sweep of all unprincipled factional struggles. We must combat individualism and sectarianism so as to enable our whole Party to march in step and fight for one common goal.

Our comrades must understand that we study Marxism-Leninism not for display, nor because there is any mystery about it, but solely because it is the science which leads the revolutionary cause of the proletariat to victory.
"Rectify the Party's Style of Work" (1942)

In class society, everyone lives as a member of a particular class, and every kind of thinking, without exception, is stamped with the brand of a class.
On Practice (1937)

If a man wants to succeed in his work, that is, to achieve the anticipated results, he must bring his ideas into correspondence with the laws of the objective external world; if they do not correspond, he will fail in his practice. After he fails, he draws his lessons, corrects his ideas to make them correspond to the laws of the external world, and can thus turn failure into success; this is what is meant by "failure is the mother of success" and "a fall into the pit, a gain in your wit.
On Practice (1937)

The Marxist philosophy of dialectical materialism has two outstanding characteristics. One is its class nature: it openly avows that dialectical materialism is in the service of the proletariat. The other is its practicality: it emphasizes the dependence of theory on practice, emphasizes that theory is based on practice and in turn serves practice.
On Practice (1937)

Whoever wants to know a thing has no way of doing so except by coming into contact with it, that is, by living (practicing) in its environment. ... If you want knowledge, you must take part in the practice of changing reality. If you want to know the taste of a pear, you must change the pear by eating it yourself.... If you want to know the theory and methods of revolution, you must take part in revolution. All genuine knowledge originates in direct experience.
On Practice (1937)

Only those who are subjective, one-sided and superficial in their approach to problems will smugly issue orders or directives the moment they arrive on the scene, without considering the circumstances, without viewing things in their totality (their history and their present state as a whole) and without getting to the essence of things (their nature and the internal relations between one thing and another). Such people are bound to trip and fall.
On Practice (1937)

Knowledge begins with practice, and theoretical knowledge, which is acquired through practice, must then return to practice. The active function of knowledge manifests itself not only in the active leap from perceptual to rational knowledge, but - and this is more important - it must manifest itself in the leap from rational knowledge to revolutionary practice.
On Practice (1937)

If we have a correct theory but merely prate about it, pigeonhole it and do not put it into practice, then that theory, however good, is of no significance.
On Practice (1937)

Marxist philosophy holds that the most important problem does not lie in understanding the laws of the objective world and thus being able to explain it, but in applying the knowledge of these laws actively to change the world.
On Practice (1937)

Discover the truth through practice, and again through practice verify and develop the truth. Start from perceptual knowledge and actively develop it into rational knowledge; then start from rational knowledge and actively guide revolutionary practice to change both the subjective and the objective world. Practice, knowledge, again practice, and again knowledge. This form repeats itself in endless cycles, and with each cycle the content of practice and knowledge rises to a higher level. Such is the whole of the dialectical-materialist theory of knowledge, and such is the dialectical-materialist theory of the unity of knowing and doing.
On Practice (1937)

Liberalism is extremely harmful in a revolutionary collective. It is a corrosive which eats away unity, undermines cohesion causes apathy and creates dissension. It robs the revolutionary ranks of compact organization and strict discipline, prevents policies from being carried through and alienates the Party organization from the masses which the Party leads. It is an extremely bad tendency.
Combat Liberalism (1937)

People who are liberals look upon the principles of Marxism as abstract dogma. They approve of Marxism, but are not prepared to practice it or to practice it in full; they are no prepared to replace their liberalism by Marxism. These people have their Marxism, but they have their liberalism as well - they talk Marxism but practice liberalism; they apply Marxism to others but liberalism to themselves. They keep both kind of goods in stock and find a use for each. This is how the minds of certain people work.
Combat Liberalism (1937)

All loyal, honest, active and upright Communists must unite to oppose the liberal tendencies shown by certain people among us, and set them on the right path. This is one of the tasks on our ideological front.
Combat Liberalism (1937)

Opposition and struggle between ideas of different kinds constantly occur within the Party; this is a reflection within the Party of contradictions between classes and between the new and the old in society. If there were no contradictions in the Party and no ideological struggles to resolve them, the Party's life would come to an end.
On Contradiction (1937)

The fundamental cause of the development of a thing is not external but internal; it lies in the contradictoriness within the thing. This internal contradiction exists in every single thing, hence its motion and development. Contradictoriness within a thing is the fundamental cause of its development, while its interrelations and interactions with other things are secondary causes.
On Contradiction (1937)

Changes in society are due chiefly to the development of the internal contradictions in society, that is, the contradiction between the productive forces and the relations of production, the contradiction between classes and the contradiction between the old and the new; it is the development of these contradictions that pushes society forward and gives the impetu6 for the suppression of the old society by the new.
On Contradiction (1937)

It [materialist dialectics] holds that external causes are the condition of change and internal causes are the basis of change, and that external causes become operative through internal causes. In a suitable temperature an egg changes into a chicken, but no temperature can change a stone into a chicken, because each has a different basis.
On Contradiction (1937)

Opposition and struggle between ideas of different kinds constantly occur within the Party; this is a reflection within the Party of contradictions between classes and between the new and the old in society. If there were no contradictions in the Party and no ideological struggles to resolve them, the Party's life would come to an end.
On Contradiction (1937)

If in any process there are a number of contradictions, one of them must be the principal contradiction playing the leading and decisive role, while the rest occupy a secondary and subordinate position. Therefore, in studying any complex process in which there are two or more contradictions, we must devote every effort to finding its principal contradiction. Once this principal contradiction is grasped, all problems can be readily solved.
On Contradiction (1937)

Of the two contradictory aspects, one must be principal and the other secondary. The principal aspect is the one playing the leading role in the contradiction. The nature of a thing is determined mainly by the principal aspect of a contradiction, the aspect that has gained the dominant position. But this situation is not static; the principal and the non-principal aspects of a contradiction transform themselves into each other and the nature of the thing changes accordingly.
On Contradiction (1937)

While we recognize that in the general development of history the material determines the mental and social being determines social consciousness, we also - and indeed must - recognize the reaction of mental on material things, of social consciousness on social being and of the superstructure on the economic base. This does not go against materialism; on the contrary, it avoids mechanical materialism and firmly upholds dialectical materialism.
On Contradiction (1937)

Contradiction and struggle are universal and absolute, but the methods of resolving contradictions, that is, the forms of struggle, differ according to the differences in the nature of the contradictions. Some contradictions are characterized by open antagonism and others are not. In accordance with the concrete development of things, some contradictions, which were originally non-antagonistic, develop into antagonistic ones, while others which were originally antagonistic develop into non-antagonistic ones.
On Contradiction (1937)

Revolutions and revolutionary wars are inevitable in class society, and without them it is impossible to accomplish any leap in social development and to overthrow the reactionary ruling classes and therefore impossible for the people to win political power.
On Contradiction (1937)

All contradictory things are interconnected; not only do they coexist in a single entity in given conditions, but in other given conditions, they also transform themselves into each other. This is the full meaning of the identity of opposites. This is what Lenin meant when he discussed "how they happen to be (how they become) identical--under what conditions they are identical, transforming themselves into one another".
On Contradiction (1937)

Qualitatively different contradictions can only be resolved by qualitatively different methods.
On Contradiction (1937)

As regards the sequence in the movement of man's knowledge, there is always a gradual growth from the knowledge of individual and particular things to the knowledge of things in general. Only after man knows the particular essence of many different things can he proceed to generalization and know the common essence of things.
On Contradiction (1937)

Opposition and struggle between ideas of different kinds constantly occur within the Party; this is a reflection within the Party of contradictions between classes and between the new and the old in society. If there were no contradictions in the Party and no ideological struggles to resolve them, the Party's life would come to an end.
On Contradiction (1937)

Every difference in men's concepts should be regarded as reflecting an objective contradiction. Objective contradictions are reflected in subjective thinking, and this process constitutes the contradictory movement of concepts, pushes forward the development of thought, and ceaselessly solves problems in man's thinking.
On Contradiction (1937)

Before it explodes, a bomb is a single entity in which opposites coexist in given conditions. The explosion takes place only when a new condition, ignition, is present. An analogous situation arises in all those natural phenomena which finally assume the form of open conflict to resolve old contradictions and produce new things.
On Contradiction (1937)

Our agrarian revolution has been a process in which the landlord class owning the land is transformed into a class that has lost its land, while the peasants who once lost their land are transformed into small holders who have acquired land, and it will be such a process once again. In given conditions having and not having, acquiring and losing, are interconnected; there is identity of the two sides. Under socialism, private peasant ownership is transformed into the public ownership of socialist agriculture; this has already taken place in the Soviet Union, as it will take place everywhere else. There is a bridge leading from private property to public property, which in philosophy is called identity, or transformation into each other, or interpenetration.
On Contradiction (1937)

The fact is that no contradictory aspect can exist in isolation. Without its opposite aspect, each loses the condition for its existence
On Contradiction (1937)

As already mentioned, so long as classes exist, contradictions between correct and incorrect ideas in the Communist Party are reflections within the Party of class contradictions. At first, with regard to certain issues, such contradictions may not manifest themselves as antagonistic. But with the development of the class struggle, they may grow and become antagonistic. The history of the Communist Party of the Soviet Union shows us that the contradictions between the correct thinking of Lenin and Stalin and the fallacious thinking of Trotsky, Bukharin and others did not at first manifest themselves in an antagonistic form, but that later they did develop into antagonism.
On Contradiction (1937)

In the new-democratic republic under the leadership of the proletariat, the state enterprises will be of a socialist character and will constitute the leading force in the whole national economy, but the republic will neither confiscate capitalist private property in general nor forbid the development of such capitalist production as does not "dominate the livelihood of the people", for China's economy is still very backward.
On New Democracy (1940)

Enterprises, such as banks, railways and airlines, whether Chinese-owned or foreign-owned, which are either monopolistic in character or too big for private management, shall be operated and administered by the state, so that private capital cannot dominate the livelihood of the people: this is the main principle of the regulation of capital.
On New Democracy (1940)

The culture of New Democracy should likewise be "shared by all the common people", that is, it should be a national, scientific and mass culture, and must under no circumstances be a culture "privately owned by the few".
Mao Tse-tung: An Anthology of his Writings (1954)

The state structure of New Democracy should be based on democratic centralism, with the people's congresses at various levels determining the major policies and electing the government. It is at once democratic and centralised, i.e. centralised on the basis of democracy and democratic under centralised guidance.
Mao Tse-tung: An Anthology of his Writings (1954)

Some Facts about Mao Zedong

Mao Zedong was born on 26 December 1893 in a village near Shaoshan in the central Chinese province of Hunan.

His father Mao Yichang (1870-1920) was the 20th generation of the Mao clan and traced his descent back to the army leader Mao Taihua, who fought against the Mongols until 1368 and settled in the region of today's Xiangtan after the establishment of the Ming Dynasty.

Mao's father had only two years of school education, was hard and diligent. He managed to free himself from the debts his father had left him. With the money he had saved during his service in the army, he bought between 15 and 20 mu of land, which he farmed with the help of farmworkers.

Later he became a wholesaler who, despite hunger, bought rice in Shaoshan and resold it to the big cities.

Mao's mother Wen Qimei (1867-1919) came from a neighboring town of Shaoshan. She had married Mao's father when he was 15 years old. Of her seven children, only three survived childhood. She was very religious, and her Buddhism influenced Mao Zedong for his whole life.

According to local standards at the time, the Maos were a wealthy farming family in their day.

The father Mao, who wanted to turn his son into a learned man and gave him the name Zedong (benefactor of the East), sent him to a private Confucian school in Shaoshan. Mao learned the material thereby heart, but the ethical and moral concepts remained foreign to him.

Mao's grandfather had fought in the Taiping Uprising, considered the most terrible war of the 19th century.

Mao experienced the effects of the Ping-Liu-Li uprising and the insecurity spread by the activities of secret societies such as Gelaohui. This and his father's despotism made Mao a rebellious child.

At the beginning of 1911, Mao went to Changsha, 70 km away - at that time a transshipment point for goods and news from all over the world - to attend a new school there.

After the news of the successful Wuchang uprising reached Changsha, Mao's school was closed. The province declared itself independent, Mao joined the Hunan army, but without a military mission. However, Mao saw the bodies of the leaders of the local uprising, Jiao Defeng, and Chen Zuoxin - his first contact with power politics.

He left the army again and tried various schools until he was accepted at the Hunan Province Teacher Training Institute in the spring of 1913.

Although he was industrious only in the subjects that interested him, the teachers respected him. In 1917 he was appointed the best pupil of the school.

He founded an association of students from Xiangtan and became chairman of the student association. In this capacity, he revived the evening school for workers.

In November 1917, he organized volunteers to defend the school from marauding soldiers with the help of the police.

In April 1918, he co-founded the New People's Study Society, in which He Shuheng also participated. This association aimed to renew China and the whole world.

The first writings of Mao Zedong date back to this time. They show Mao's admiration for Shang Yang, the theories of vitalism and the power of human will, but also the successful provincial governor Zeng Guofan. Among those Chinese who wanted to save their country from Western colonization efforts at the time, these were prevalent views.

When Mao finished school, he had high ambitions but was disoriented. During his school days, he had developed a friendship with teacher Yang Changji, who strongly influenced Mao's viewpoints and drew his attention to radical positions such as those of Miyazaki Tōten.

Unlike other politicians of his time, Mao did not attend any of the newly founded universities. He worked out his positions on his own in the Changsha City Library. He remained more deeply rooted in cultural traditions than other later communist revolutionaries.

At the age of 13, Mao left school because of the teacher's violence. Since the examinations for civil servants had been abolished and education no longer automatically meant entry into the imperial bureaucracy, his father hoped that Mao would help in his father's business. Against his father's will, however, Mao mainly read, for example, the works of the influential reformer Zheng Guanying.

At the age of 16, Mao and his 9-year-old cousin began attending a school that taught modern subjects. However, he only stayed at this school for one year because he suffered from the hatred and arrogance of his classmates: he was marginalized because of his peasant background and the dialect of the Xiang language spoken in his home village.

At the age of fourteen, Mao was married to the eighteen-year-old Luo Yigu, whose clan was linked to the Mao family through distant family ties. Mao rejected this marriage and hid with a friend in Shaoshan, Luo Yigu died as early as 1910.

Mao's teacher and friend Yang Changji was appointed to Beijing University in 1918. In mid-1918, Yang suggested that Mao and some classmates join the Worker Student Program and go to France.

Mao went to Beijing with 25 classmates to Yang in August 1918. Through his teacher, he found employment as an assistant librarian, where he met Li Dazhao, one of the most important early Chinese Marxists and co-founder of the Chinese Communist Party. Li was an editor of the journal Neue Jugend, which shaped the political and intellectual direction of the fourth May movement; he introduced Mao to the ideas of Marxism and Bolshevism.

He also made the acquaintance of Chen Duxiu here, through whom he gained access to anarchist and Trotskyist ideas.

He also spent much time in Beijing studying on his own, reading numerous articles on the topics of his time.

At the end of his stay in Beijing, however, Mao was closest to Hu Shi and his philosophical pragmatism.

During his stay in Beijing, Mao decided not to go to France. In April 1919 he was back in Hunan, not least because of his mother's illness.

Mao initially stayed in Changsha, where he was already an accepted leader, whereas he had been widely ignored in Beijing.

While he was working as a primary school teacher, China suffered a foreign policy defeat: the Paris Peace Conference of 1919 decided that the German colonies in China would be handed over to Japan.

Mao probably did not take part in the subsequent demonstrations of the Fourth May Movement, but together with friends, he organized a boycott of Japanese goods.

He founded a student newspaper called Xiangjiang Pinglun with similar contents to Chen Duxius' publication. It caused a national sensation, was printed in the relatively large edition of 5,000 copies, the 5th edition of which was published in the same format as the first.

Mao's early writings show an orientation towards the communist anarchism of Pyotr Alexeyevich Kropotkin, Mao's commitment to the abolition of Confucian constraints and women's rights, and view that more justice can only be achieved peacefully because if one tries to eliminate oppression through oppression, there will be oppression again in the end.

During winter 1919, Mao traveled to Beijing again to get the central government to remove Governor Zhang Jingyao, who were plundering Hunan province, but without success. During his stay, Mao often met with Li Dazhao and Deng Zhongxia and read the Marxist works available in Chinese translation.

From May 1920 Mao stayed in Shanghai, where he worked and promoted Hunan's independence from China, a constitution, and democratic elections. Chen Duxiu, who had meanwhile fled Beijing to Shanghai and was in contact with the Comintern, tried to talk him out of these ideas.

After his return to Changsha - Zhang had been overthrown in the meantime - Mao got a job as headmaster of a primary school.

Besides, he opened a bookshop for political literature at affordable prices and founded a society to study Russia.

Towards the end of the year, he concluded that Bolshevism was the right ideology because it was radical. From then on, Mao saw himself as a Marxist and was guided by Marxism and the history of the October Revolution. He began by founding underground cells of the Socialist Youth League in Changsha.

In July 1921, Mao participated in the 1st Party Congress of the Communist Party of China (CPC) as one of the two representatives of the Changsha cell.

The party had only 53 members at the time, and the possibility of seizure of power was a long way off. Mao took the minutes at this congress and was not very active apart from that. The Comintern representatives at this congress explained how power should be seized in backward countries and colonies, but Mao did not understand this tactic, just like the other Chinese participants.

In Changsha Mao together with Li Lisan, whom Mao had met at school, he founded trade unions, although there were fewer workers in Hunan in the sense of Karl Marx.

In 1922 he organized several powerful strikes, for example in Anyuan, where Mao went several times to organize the miners and railway workers of the coal mines. These strikes led to significant economic improvements for the workers.

As chairman of the Hunan Trade Union Federation, Mao was the negotiating partner of Provincial Governor Zhao Hengti. With the governor's money, he founded a school to train cadres of the CP.

Mao traveled again to Shanghai for the 2nd Party Congress, but forgot the venue and therefore did not attend the Congress.

In the autumn of 1919, Mao had an affair with his former classmate Tao Yi, which, however, broke up due to different political views.

From September 1920 he met the daughter of his late teacher and friend Yang Changji, Yang Kaihui. After initial shyness, they married in the winter of 1920 without a bridal gift and Chinese ceremony; love marriages were not the norm at the time. It was not until October 1921 that they were able to move into a common apartment.

In January 1923, the central executive committee of the CPC decided to bring Mao to the headquarters in Shanghai. It was high time for this because the warlord Wu Peifu had begun to fight the trade unions by force and Governor Zhao Hengti had announced Mao for arrest and execution.

Mao traveled via Shanghai to Canton, where the 3rd Party Congress took place in June. At this congress, at the request of the Comintern, the First United Front was enforced, and Mao was elected in the nine-member executive committee of the CP and head of the organizational department of the First United Front. Mao was divided on the policy of the united front, and in the end, he supported it: He realized that all democratic forces would have to unite to put an end to the era of the warlords.

His efforts to found cells for the Kuomintang (KMT) from Shanghai were unsuccessful. At the end of December 1924, he asked for release for health reasons; the never-ending frictions between the CP and Kuomintang, as well as the constant interference and frequent personnel and policy changes of the Comintern, had afflicted him.

Mao spent most of 1925 in his native Shaoshan. There he began to organize the local farmers and to take an interest in communism. Although he had previously had only contempt for the rural population, he realized here that a revolution in China could only be successful if it relied on the countless impoverished peasants.

In the summer Mao had to flee Hunan again because he had instructed starving peasants to force a wholesaler to sell the rice at acceptable prices.

He went to Canton and began working at the recently established Whampoa Military Academy.

In mid-March, he was appointed a director of the Institute for the Formation of the Peasant Movement, which allowed him to focus exclusively on mobilizing the rural population and become an expert on the peasant movement within the CPC. The many peasants who had no better alternative than to fight their way through in gangs, as beggars, or as mercenaries in one of the armies of the warlords, Mao increasingly regarded them as potential allies of the CP. Repeatedly, he was released from his obligations in Canton to investigate the situation of the peasants.

In the course of the northern campaign, Mao was transferred back to Shanghai, where he led the working group for mobilizing the peasants with high activity and extensive travel. Mao hoped that the end of the warlords' rule would also mean the end of the lords of the manor. Again, he was involved in the problematic maneuvering between the CPC, Comintern, and Kuomintang.

In early 1927, he returned to Hunan, where he researched the status of the peasant movement. The extensive report on an investigation into the peasant movement in Hunan, which he presented to the party leadership after his return, was adopted, published several times in China, and partially published in English and Russian in the Communist International newspaper. From here, Mao assumed a violent revolution by the peasantry.

The first united front finally broke up in mid-May when Chiang Kai-shek had killed numerous Communists in Shanghai, and three days later a blow was struck against the Communists in Canton Shanghai. Mao was in Wuhan at the time, trying to resolve the issue of land distribution within the Kuomintang. However, he resigned himself by stating that the Kuomintang leadership was not interested in a solution and that it was only making big words.

At this point, the KPC was in a hopeless situation. On a short trip to Hunan, Mao concluded that the CPC could only succeed in the struggle for power if it had its military. Political conflict, mass movement, and a united front are pointless because, in militarized China of the 1920s, all political power comes from gun barrels.

According to Mao, such a communist army should be recruited from impoverished peasants the Comintern only conditionally approved Mao's proposal to establish communist bases in hard-to-reach areas. It now relied on uprisings against the Kuomintang, in whose planning Mao was involved as an expert on mobilizing peasants.

Mao was not involved in the Nanchang Uprising on August 1, 1927.

On August 7 he took part in the Extraordinary Conference of the Central Committee of the CPC, where the new Comintern representative Bessarion Lominadse and Mao criticized Chen Duxiu's policy as too little radical.

After the conference, Mao was again to work for the party in Shanghai, but he insisted on organizing an autumn uprising in Hunan to implement his concept of creating liberated zones in the agrarian hinterland. In Mao's opinion, the entire land should be transferred to joint ownership, although he had to be aware that the peasants did not want this.

In August 1927 Mao was sent to Hunan to carry out the autumn harvest uprising. The Comintern wanted to take the provincial capital of Changsha, but Mao was not convinced of this strategy. He headed the Front Committee, which dealt with the military issues of the uprising.

The uprising on September 9, in which peasants, railway workers, and miners were to participate, was quickly crushed. Mao narrowly escaped execution, so that Mao and the members of the Hunan CP committee decided not to attack Changsha.

Instead, Mao moved with about 1500 soldiers towards the Jinggang Mountains, where they arrived at the end of October.

An assembly of representatives of the workers, peasants and soldiers as the legislative branch and a people's assembly as the executive branch were established. Mao had to come to terms with the leaders of the local gang called the Forest Brotherhood, who controlled the region. Yuan Wencai, one of these bandit leaders, paired Mao with He Zizhen to secure his loyalty.

While Mao was in the mountains, the KP shrank considerably under the pressure of the Kuomintang. Numerous Communists retreated to the countryside. Mao was condemned for his "military opportunism" and removed from the Politburo.
For him, this marked the beginning of fighting with rivals within the CP who regarded Mao's troops as ordinary bandits.

In April 1928, the remaining troops of the Nanchang uprising commanded by Zhu De arrived in Mao-controlled territory. Zhu and Mao agreed to jointly establish a Soviet capital Longshi, implement land reform, and arm the masses.

By the end of the year, an egalitarian, militarized society based on terror against the individual and necessarily financed by looting and opium trafficking was established in the Jinggang Mountains.

In May 1928, Zhu and Mao commanded some 18,000 poorly trained, undisciplined and malnourished fighters, a third of whom were ill or wounded. The troops owned a total of about 2000 rifles.

Until November 1928, the entire country land was confiscated and redistributed against considerable resistance from the peasants. The failure of the autumn uprising had shown that the local elites had a very high influence on the poor peasants. For this reason, the people around Mao took very hard action against the rich peasants and landlords.

At the CP's 6th Congress in June and July 1928, held in Moscow, Mao's ideas were sharply criticized. Nevertheless, he was elected in absentia to the Central Committee of the CP - after all, he was the only one who could create and maintain a communist basis.

Among the criticisms of Mao were the question of land distribution and the treatment of wealthy peasants in the context of land reform. Party headquarters feared that it would lose control of Mao and Zhu and that the two would become warlords. It instructed Mao and Zhu to hand over the army command and divide the Red Army into smaller units; Mao ignored these instructions. The Comintern turned in parallel to Mao's line of guerrilla combat.

In December 1928 the troops of Peng Dehuai arrived in the Jinggang Mountains. It was clear that the region was so unproductive, but also so plundered, that it could not keep the soldiers, and that the Jinggang Soviet had failed.

In January 1929, the communist base was therefore relocated to southeast Jiangxi, on the border with Fujian, contrary to the party's wishes. In this phase, Mao Zedong again became a father, since Mao, his wife and the army was on the run from Kuomintang persecutors, daughter Jinhua had to be left with peasants half an hour after her birth.

The regime that Mao and Zhu established in their new base did not differ significantly from that in Jinggangshan. A land reform was also carried out in southeastern Jiangxi, whereby the guidelines of the Comintern and deculacization were applied.

The arrival of numerous officials and Comintern advisers trained in the Soviet Union led to intense conflicts. Mao was criticized over the cadres, which had no idea of grassroots work and only dogmas from the books attached.

Also between Zhu and Mao conflicts intensified in the first half of 1929 around the correct guidance of the Soviet. From June to November 1929, Mao therefore withdrew due to illness and depression until the Central Committee took his side.

At the beginning of November 1934, the Communists with almost 90,000 men left for the West with an unknown destination. The mood among the fighters was bad, the Red Army resembled a band of defeated ones. Mao used the mood and the long rides to draw Luo Fu, later Wang Jiaxiang and Zhou Enlai to his side from Bo Gus' circle of supporters.

He had the advantage of being able to repudiate any blame for the loss of the Jiangxi Soviet. His name thus stood for a new beginning. On the first important vote on the Long March, namely the one about the goal of the evacuation, he was able to assert himself and the mountainous terrain of Guangxi, Guizhou and Sichuan was chosen.

In January 1935, the Red Army stopped marching in Zunyi, and the party leadership met for a discussion at the three-day Zunyi conference. Bo Gu and Zhou Enlai, who had been responsible for the Communist Party military since 1932, had to report. Luo Fu and, after him, Mao Zedong, severely attacked Bo and Otto Braun in their speeches, blaming their mistakes for the loss of the Soviet. At the end of this conference, Bo Gu had no supporters other than Kai Feng and Otto Braun, while Mao was again appointed a member of the Politburo's Standing Committee.

In February, Bo had to hand over his post as secretary-general of the party to Luo Fu, and in March Mao was elected political commissioner of the newly created military council. After this conference, the trio of Luo, Wang, and Mao dominated the party. Mao had thus regained the influence and positions he had lost in 1932.

In June 1935 the Mao's First Front Army met the Fourth Front Army of Zhang Guotao. Zhang's troops were stronger and better equipped, while the Red Army had practically lost its combat readiness. The political leadership of the First Front Army, on the other hand, was legitimized by Moscow.

Zhang and Mao also had a personal dislike for each other. The inevitable power struggle between Zhang and Mao came about; Mao risked a new division of the communist camp. He wanted to move north to jointly establish a Soviet territory extend it to the border with the Soviet Union. He also wanted to take up the fight against the Japanese invasion to legitimize his claim to leadership over Zhang Guotao with the argument of fighting for national sovereignty.

On 22 October 1935, Mao declared the Long March in the north of Shaanxi province to be over. Here Mao's army was united with Liu Zhidan's Bao' an Soviet troops.

The Long March had enabled Mao to take power over the party, but the Red Army had shrunk to 5000 soldiers.

After return to Soviet politics, the party was on the Li-Lisan line, a much more aggressive course. In the summer of 1930, Zhu and Mao and their troops had to attack the cities of Jiujiang and Nanchang at the request of the CP headquarters, and both operations failed.

The city of Changsha was captured and held for a few days, which prompted the Kuomintang to execute Mao's wife Yang Kaihui, and the losses to the Red Army were enormous.

The army now had 54,000 soldiers, but hardly any equipment. Mao's insight from these developments was that the Soviet had to build proper government bodies. In October 1930, therefore, the barely defended city of Ji'an was captured, and the Soviet government of Jiangxi province proclaimed. A year later, on November 7, 1931, the First Congress of the Chinese Soviets was held in Ruijin. Mao was elected chairman of the All-China Executive Committee and chairman of the People's Commissioners Council. Ruijin was proclaimed the capital of the Chinese Soviet republic.

In mid-April 1932, Mao succeeded in having the Soviet government declared war on Japan in the hope of winning the sympathy of patriotic Chinese.

Parallel to these events, Comintern representative Pawel Mif arrived in Shanghai and began to rebuild the CP leadership at will. Since the Kuomintang simultaneously infiltrated provocateurs and spies into the Communist Party and launched an attack on the Soviet with 100,000 soldiers, the party's internal struggles reached their temporary climax with the Futian incident. This wave of cleansing cost more than 1000 Communists their lives. At the time, Mao did not know that Stalin had been protecting him since the late 1920s and supporting him with propaganda. Nevertheless, Mao lost influence in the party and army. Once again, he retreated to the mountains; Bo Gu took control of the party. Otto Braun replaced Mao Zedong's guerrilla strategy of repulsing four Kuomintang attacks with positional warfare, as taught at Soviet military academies.

In the summer of 1934, the situation was hopeless, preparations for evacuation were made. Mao learned of this only a few days before the march when he was with the First Red Army Corps near Yudu, 60 km west of Ruijin.

Mao's wife, He Zizhen, was allowed to take part in the Long March, his then two-year-old son Anhong had to stay behind and has been missing ever since.

In the months following his arrival in North Shaanxi, Mao reorganized the Red Army, which now had about 10,000 fighters. The strategy of presenting the Red Army as an anti-Japanese army began to take effect. The December 9, 1935 movement, which had demanded stronger action against Japanese aggression from the Nanjing government, led to an increased influx into the CP.

Mao Zedong's approach was in line with that of Moscow, even though the contact there was temporarily severed: Stalin wanted a stable China to secure the Soviet Union against Japan. He, therefore, instructed the Communist Party to strive for a united front with the Kuomintang. Mao also sought a consensus with his former opponents. In December 1935, the party decided that the national bourgeoisie should fight with the workers and peasants of China against the Japanese.

The Politburo meeting of 8 December 1935 accordingly formulated an appeal to the Kuomintang for a ceasefire and a joint struggle against Japan. Chiang Kai-shek, however, prompted further attacks on the Communists. The most important question now was to win at least part of the Kuomintang for a ceasefire. An opportunity for this was offered in the person of Zhang Xueliang, who had withdrawn with his troops from Manchuria in Shaanxi provincial capital Xi'an before the Japanese, and who was also looking for allies.

Already in November Mao had offered a ceasefire to a commander of Zhang's troops. In April 1936 there were direct negotiations, which resulted in a ceasefire and even arms deliveries from Zhang to the CP. For this reason, Chiang visited Zhang for a personal discussion in Xi'an. Parallel to this discussion, more than ten thousand students demonstrated against Chiang's lax Japan policy. This conversation led to Chiang's arrest.

Stalin, however, put pressure Chiang to be released. Shortly before these events, Germany and Japan had signed the Anti-Comintern Pact. Stalin now wanted a stable China more than before, and Chiang was the strongest actor. Stalin, therefore, urged Mao to resolve the conflict peacefully. Relations between Stalin and Mao came under enormous pressure, for it is evident that Chiang and his many German advisers first worked to destroy the Communist Party and then to resist Japan. Ultimately, however, the Chinese Communist Party was financially dependent on the Soviet Union. On February 10, 1937, the CP again sent a message to the 3rd plenary of the Kuomintang, in which it formulated the basis for cooperation against Japan.

From March to May 1937, pressure from Moscow led to an understanding between Kuomintang and the Communist Party on cooperation. In July 1937, the Second United Front was formally adopted. The Red Army was placed under the supreme command of the Nanjing government and was now the 8th marching army of the National Revolutionary Army commanded by Zhu De. Mao recognized the leading role of the Kuomintang; however, both sides were already planning the inner-Chinese struggle, which would continue after the end of the war against Japan.

Mao also pushed through on 22 August 1937 that the Red Army would continue to be a guerrilla army. He argued that the loss of the army would also be the end of the Communist Party and its functionaries personally. The Red Army henceforth carried out actions in Japanese-occupied territory, and the social changes in the territories controlled by the Communist Party continued.

During the Great Terror in the Soviet Union, Mao began to seek further allies. For example, he contacted the Labour Party and welcomed Evans Carlson, the confidant of American President Roosevelt. Carlson was much more positive about Mao than he was about Chiang: he described him as a dreamer and a genius. He considered the CP's policy at the time liberal-democratic and stressed that Mao was planning a coalition government for China.

In parallel, he resolved the power struggle with his opponent Wang Ming, Stalin's confidante, and China's representative in the Comintern. Wang had repeatedly sown doubts about Stalin's loyalty to Mao, Stalin demanded that Wang report any Trotskyist deviation. Since Zhang Guotao, Kang Sheng, Bo Gu, and Zhou Enlai were also on Wang Ming's line and, not least, worked closely with the Kuomintang, Mao sent his representative to Moscow with Ren Bishi.

When shortly afterward, the Comintern stressed the importance of supporting Mao Zedong as leader of the Communist Party, the leadership problem was solved. Mao's Chinese communism thus also prevailed against the communists trained in the Soviet Union.

The party's cult of leadership and Stalinization began, Mao now started to promote this cult himself actively. The reports by Edgar Snow, Agnes Smedley, and other Western journalists led to an inevitable spread of the Mao cult abroad.

In June 1936, the CP lost its headquarters in Wayaobao because of an attack by the Kuomintang and had to flee to Bao'an, a semi-deserted place with about 400 inhabitants.

In January 1937, the Central Committee of the CP moved from the Bao'an to Yan'an. He Zizhen had just born her fifth child, Li Min, and life in Yan'an, where many young people who wanted to commit themselves to communism had come, also brought with it many temptations in gender relations. The marriages of numerous party officials were divorced. He Zizhen also left Mao after affairs with the American journalist Agnes Smedley and the Chinese actress Wu Lili.

In September 1938 Mao began an affair with the film actress Lan Ping. He married her on November 19, 1939, before he had chosen the name Jiang Qing for her. Jiang Qing was the former lover of Kang Sheng, who would later become head of the Chinese secret services and steered among other things the campaign against the right-wingers. Later they were part of the Gang of Four. Their daughter Li Na was born on 3 August 1940.

In July 1937, Mao began to engage intensively with Marxist and Bolshevik philosophy and to give lectures at the newly founded Anti-Japanese Military Political University. He has also published numerous reflections on political and military issues and transferred the ideology of Marxism to Chinese culture and reality. This turn to Marxism was tolerated by Stalin, who knew that Mao also had to show intellectual achievements in order to establish a cult of leadership in China.

In order to broaden support among the population and out of concern for the cohesion of the Communist Party, Mao, together with Chen Boda, developed the concept of New Democracy at the end of 1939. It included state respect for property, promotion of Chinese entrepreneurship, promotion of foreign investment, state control of key sectors, a multi-party system with a coalition government, and democratic freedoms. To foreign visitors, Mao declared that the New Democracy was a necessary intermediate step for China on the path to socialism and, ultimately, communism. When it became apparent that the Communists would win the civil war, Mao turned away from this concept. However, it had led to a secession of left-wing groups within the Kuomintang under the leadership of Sun Yatsen's widow Song Qingling.

With the establishment of liberated areas behind the Japanese lines, the number of members of the Communist Party grew very rapidly. Between 1935 and 1945, 44 party schools were established in the base area of Yan'an alone to train and socialize new members and to exercise ideological control. In addition, meetings began to be convened where self-criticism was expected and practiced by the participants. Training courses and self-incrimination campaigns were organized. Under Kang Sheng, the first special commissions were set up.

At the party conference in Yan'an in 1945, 754 delegates took part, representing 1.2 million members in the meantime. At this congress of unity - Wang Ming had meanwhile been dismantled, Zhou Enlai was no threat to Mao's claim to leadership - a new party statute was passed in which Mao Zedong thinking was declared the basis of the Chinese Communist Party. Mao was now the supreme leader of the communist movement and held all power in his hands. His earlier positions, which had often earned him an outsider role, were now declared the central CP line, and the policies formerly pursued by the majority of the CP were declared minority positions. A Committee for the Purification of History was given the explicit mandate to adapt history to the necessities of the cult.

After the Japanese attack on Pearl Harbour, it was clear to Mao that the U.S. would have to defeat Japan and the Communists would have to spare their forces for the ensuing war against the Kuomintang. Mao, therefore, welcomed Dixie Mission, with which the USA wanted to have a team led by David D. Barrett and John S. Service investigate the Communists. He was able to convey to US representatives that the U.S. was the only country that could help China achieve its goal of rapid economic growth.

In order to prevent the U.S. from donating its aid to the Kuomintang, Mao even considered renaming the Communist Party. The image that the participants in the Dixie mission painted was quite positive. But he was received with skepticism by large sections of the American secret services. The American government was not deceived.

Shortly before Japan surrendered, the Chinese Civil War flared up again. Negotiations between Mao and Chiang did not produce any results. The US Ambassador Patrick J. Hurley tried to mediate between the CP and Kuomintang in an understanding and accompanied Mao to Chongqing on 28 August 1945. The talks were to last six weeks. Chiang Kai-shek, however, remained unwilling to cooperate with the Communists. In the same month, Chiang signed a friendship and alliance treaty with the Kuomintang. After the capitulation, the Kuomintang controlled two-thirds of Chinese territory, while the Communists held some liberated areas with the center in the border area of Shaanxi, Gansu, and Ningxia. In total, 95.5 million people lived in the Communist-controlled areas. Japanese soldiers were ordered to surrender only to Kuomintang soldiers; Japanese captured soldiers were used in activities against the Communists. In this way, the Kuomintang was able to strongly repress the Red Army until 1947. The Yan'an base also had to be abandoned. Mao instructed the Red Army troops only to engage in combat if their victory was certain, and to apply guerrilla tactics exclusively.

Despite Chiang's 1947 offensive on the Yan'an base and Stalin's reluctance to supply arms and transfer money - his mistrust of Mao had grown and he did not want to provoke the US - the People's Liberation Army grew from 1.2 to 3.5 million soldiers within a year.

In the summer of 1947, the Red Army implemented Mao's plan to occupy the Dabie Mountains in central China. This destroyed all of Chiang's plans and forced him to massively move troops. The influx to the People's Liberation Army and Chiang Kai-shek's mistakes led Mao to unite his forces with those of Liu Shaoqi and Zhu De in Xibaipo in May 1948. While Chiang's troops increasingly disintegrated due to corruption and the pursuit of personal interests by commanders, the Red Army fighters were fanatical.

In January 1949, they succeeded in capturing Manchuria, and a few months later Beijing, Shanghai, and Nanjing were conquered. Until 1950, all of China was occupied by the Communists. On October 1, 1949, Mao Zedong proclaimed the People's Republic of China at the Gate of Tiananmen and now faced the task of stabilizing the new state and its unity. He led a coalition government as chairman, Liu Shaoqi, Zhu De and Song Qingling were his deputies.

In the founding phase of the People's Republic, Mao was already 56 years old and his health was under attack. He suffered from insomnia and sometimes a loss of orientation. Nevertheless, he worked 15 to 16 hours a day, mainly at night. From September 1949 he lived in Zhongnanhai, where he lived with his relatives in a traditional courtyard. Apart from political relations, he had no friendships.

His wife Jiang Qing organized his daily routine, Mao's only pleasures were dance performances, for which Jiang Qing organized young dance partners.

He preferred to welcome his staff and guests in his bedroom with a huge bed from which he organized the new state.

Contrary to Stalin's advice, Mao had chosen Beijing as the new capital of China, although he originally abhorred the decadence of the Qing Dynasty. The fundamental changes planned for Beijing - including the demolition of the Forbidden City - were not implemented because of the political turmoil in the young People's Republic. The concept of the New Democracy now gave way to the democratic dictatorship of the people.

Already in 1948, Mao planned to visit Stalin with his economists Ren Bishi and Chen Yun. Stalin canceled this visit again and again. Only in December 1949 did Mao travel to Moscow on the occasion of Stalin's 70th birthday. A three-month stay was planned, which was Mao's first trip abroad. For security reasons Mao traveled by train - soldiers with machine guns were posted every 50 meters. With the exception of two receptions, however, Stalin largely ignored Mao. Mao was disappointed and felt deported to the "Lipki" dacha. Stalin initially rejected Mao's wish to terminate the friendship treaty with the Kuomintang government, which was advantageous for the Soviet Union. It was only towards the end of the visit that an agreement on friendship, alliance and mutual assistance was reached, but in its secret annexes, China granted the Soviet Union privileges in Xinjiang and Manchuria. In addition, joint ventures in mining and heavy industry under Soviet leadership were planned, and China did not regain control of railways in Manchuria and the military port of Lüshun for the time being.

Mao was very angry at what he perceived as Soviet imperialism. However, Stalin distrusted Mao, whom he had repeatedly called a "cave Marxist," and saw in a strengthening China potential competition for his hegemony in the Communist camp. Mao, however, was largely dependent on Stalin. At Mao's request, Stalin sent his Marxist expert Pawel Judin to China, who spent two years examining Mao's works and confirming that Mao was a Marxist. But Mao had also noticed Stalin's physical weakness in Moscow.

Mao knew already in 1949 - the Chinese civil war was not yet over - about Kim Il-sung's plans to attack the militarily much weaker South Korea. In view of the numerous Korean participants in the liberation of Manchuria, Mao promised Kim Chinese support for these plans.

In spring and May 1950, Mao promised Kim to help him with the three Korean divisions of the People's Liberation Army and, if necessary, with Chinese "volunteer associations. Neither Kim nor Mao knew at the time that Stalin wanted to provoke the USA's entry into the Korean War in order to bind the forces of both the USA and China in the longer term. Mao was of the opinion that the USA would not risk a major war because of such a small area as South Korea.

After North Korea had almost completely conquered South Korea by October 1950, UN troops under American leadership succeeded in throwing North Korean troops back and bringing them to the brink of defeat. Mao hesitated to send his troops to war under these circumstances. He wrote to Stalin that the war in Korea would thwart all plans for the peaceful reconstruction of China. Most of the rest of the Chinese leadership, including Zhou Enlai and Lin Biao, were also against the war.

Stalin wiped Mao's concerns from the table, but refused direct Soviet support for Kim. On October 5, Peng Dehuai argued in the Politburo's expanded plenary that China must avoid an American-controlled Korea. The decision to enter the war was made. On 12 October, Mao withdrew again in a letter to Stalin, instructing Stalin to give up Kim Korea.

On 13 October Mao again agreed to send troops, so that on 19 October four field armies and three artillery divisions of the People's Liberation Army marched in. The number of war victims on the Chinese and North Korean sides quickly rose to hundreds of thousands, so that Lin Biao and Gao Gang tried in the summer of 1951 to obtain Stalin's permission for ceasefire negotiations.

In 1952, Mao even had to decide to provide food aid to North Korea despite bottlenecks in China. Stalin, however, wanted to delay the end of the war so that a ceasefire could only be achieved after Stalin's death on 27 July 1953. Economically, the war was an extreme burden for China because Stalin demanded that the Soviet loan be used to pay for Soviet arms.

During the Korean War, Mao lost his son Mao Anying, who had volunteered for the war and had been assigned to the general staff. He was killed in an American air raid. Mao took this news with outward indifference and said that a war would claim victims. Inside, however, he was badly hit, suffered from insomnia for a long time, did not eat and smoked.

In May 1956, Mao initiated the Hundred Flower Movement: he had the censorship of intellectuals loosened in order to obtain new stimuli, assuming that he had only about three percent of intellectuals against him. Out of fear of the regime, the intellectuals' criticism only began a year later in May 1957 in the course of another campaign.

Since Mao's policies were also severely criticized, Mao had the Hundred flower movement stopped by Deng Xiaoping, defamed the intellectuals in a new class struggle campaign against the right and had 300,000 of them imprisoned. Furthermore, 400,000 to 700,000 employees who appeared to him to be "enemies of the people" were dismissed and replaced by new communist cadres from the peasant classes.

In a speech to party leaders in 1958, Mao said: "What is so unusual about Emperor Shi Huangdi of the Qin dynasty? He buried only 460 scholars alive, whereas we buried 46,000 scholars alive. We are a hundred times ahead of the emperor [...] in the oppression of counterrevolutionary scholars."

The Great Leap Forward was the official slogan for the policy of the People's Republic of China from 1958 to the beginning of 1962. The goal was to industrialize China as quickly as possible. The historian and sinologist Frank Dikötter, who teaches in Hong Kong, argues with reference to the evaluation of detailed reports of the security services from these years that the Great Leap Forward is said to have caused the biggest man-made famine in history, which cost the lives of about 45 million people.

In the case of the Great Leap Forward, however, the extent to which its economic consequences have been caused by bad planning or how profound its economic consequences were themselves is increasingly controversial. Among other things, the Chinese-American economist Li Minqi argues that although the Great Leap Forward ultimately caused recession and the so-called three difficult years of 1959-1962, it had nevertheless built the infrastructure necessary for China's economic and social stability in the long term.

Deng Xiaoping, the later reform politician, did not deny his joint responsibility for the Great Leap and warned against blaming Mao. On April 1, 1980, he said: "Mao's brain was overheated at the time. But so did our heads. No one contradicted him, not even I."

The catastrophic consequences of the campaign were concealed from the population and those who dared to talk about it were eliminated.

After the detonation of the first Chinese atomic bomb in 1964 and the publication of the Small Red Book with quotations of Mao compiled by Lin Biao in 1966, the cult of personality grew around Mao. After he had lost much of his power through the failure of the Great Leap, his ideological position became increasingly incontestable.

In 1966, Mao launched the Great Proletarian Cultural Revolution by supporting critical wall newspapers and calling on schoolchildren, students and workers to break through newly established social structures. With the slogan "Love for mother and father does not resemble love for Mao Zedong," he called on children to denounce their parents as "counterrevolutionaries" or "right-wingers" - just as the promotion of denunciation of one of Mao's most effective instruments of rule was at all. The declared goal of the campaign was to eliminate reactionary tendencies among party cadres, teachers, and cultural creators. In reality, the resulting chaos was intended to bring about Mao Zedong's renewed seizure of power and the elimination of his intra-party opponents, especially Liu Shaoqi, which Mao succeeded in doing with the help of Lin Biao and the Gang of Four.

His opponents within the party were arrested for treason, killed or "re-socialized" through physical labor. The young people incited in the course of the revolution united to so-called Red Guards. In the following years, the young people trudged schools and universities, killed and maltreated numerous people, especially those with education (teachers, doctors, artists, monks, party cadres), destroyed cultural monuments, temples, libraries and museums, fought among themselves and disturbed public order lastingly.

Mao Zedong, who after the elimination of Liu Shaoqi had the power firmly under control again, called already in 1968 on the rioting youths to carry their "true revolutionary idea" into the sparsely populated peasant western provinces and to take the hard working peasants there as proletarian role models. Since only a few young people wanted to replace school-free unrest in large Chinese cities with hard field work in poor western provinces, the army had to be deployed in the following years to openly fight the Red Guards and enforce the newly introduced compulsory schooling. Subsequently, numerous Red Guards were shot dead in mass executions. The Cultural Revolution was officially declared over only after Mao's death in 1976, and the Gang of Four was held responsible for the riots.

In foreign policy terms, Mao's greatest success was the inclusion of the People's Republic of China in the United Nations in 1971. At the same time, the Republic of China in Taiwan was expelled from the UN.

The visit of US President Nixon in 1972 also contributed to the "bamboo curtain" becoming more permeable.

Made in the USA
Columbia, SC
10 May 2025